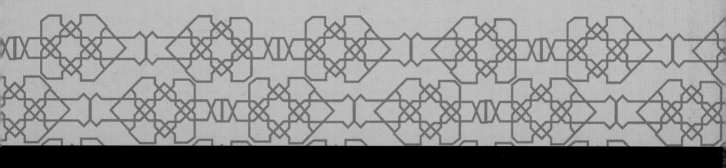

Jewish Festivals
Through the Year

Anita Ganeri

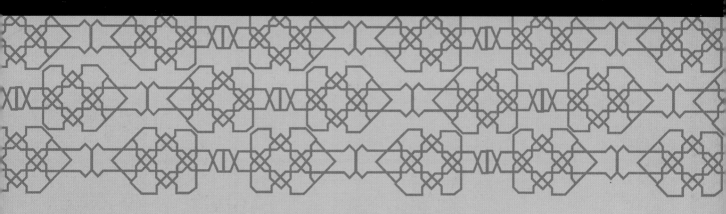

W
FRANKLIN WATTS

© 2003 Franklin Watts

First published in Great Britain by
Franklin Watts
96 Leonard Street
LONDON EC2A 4XD

Franklin Watts Australia
45–51 Huntley Street
Alexandria
NSW 2015

ISBN: 0 7496 4448 6
A CIP catalogue record for this book is available
from the British Library

Printed in Hong Kong, China

Editor: Kate Banham
Art Direction: Jonathan Hair
Educational Consultant: Alan Brown
Faith Consultant: Jonathan Gorsky,
Council for Christians and Jews

Designer: Joelle Wheelwright
Illustrations: Peter Bull
Map (page 7): Aziz Khan
Picture Research: Diana Morris

Acknowledgements
The publishers would like to thank the following for permission to
reproduce photographs in this book:
Chris Fairclough/Franklin Watts: 9t, 11; S. Grant/Trip: 12t; I.Genut/Trip: front cover,
16t, 20t, 20b, 23t; E. James/Trip: 8b, 9b; Peter Millard/Franklin Watts: 8t, 10b, 19b,
24; Muzlish/Trip: 25t, 25b; © Palphot Ltd.:10c; Zev Radovan, Jerusalem: 7b, 15b;
H.Rogers/Trip: 14b, 18b, 19t, 22 illustrations Heinz Sealig; R Seale/Trip: 6b;
S. Shapiro/Trip: 21b; Steve Shott/Franklin Watts: 17t, 26; J. Soester/Trip: 28c;
A. Tovy/Trip: 13b, 16b, 17b.

Whilst every attempt has been made to clear copyright, should there be any inadvertent
omission please apply in the first instance to the publisher regarding rectification.

Contents

Words printed in **bold** are explained in the glossary.

Introduction

Judaism is the religion of the Jewish people. Anyone born of a Jewish mother is counted as a Jew, even if they do not actively follow any religious practices. Jews believe in one God who created the world and cares for everyone and everything in it. Judaism is one of the world's oldest religions, dating back some 4,000 years.

A view of Jerusalem, the capital of Israel and a sacred city for the Jews.

Festival dates

The Jewish calendar is based on the moon. Each of the 12 months begins at the new moon and lasts for 29 or 30 days. This gives 354 days in the year. But the everyday Western calendar is based on the sun and has 365 days. Many Jewish festivals are linked to a particular season of the year. So every few years, an extra month, called *Adar 2*, is added to keep the festivals in step with the seasons. (See page 28 for the names of the Jewish months.)

Jewish beliefs

Abraham is called the father of the Jewish people. He was the leader of a group of nomadic people, called the **Hebrews**, who lived in the Middle East. Jews believe that God made a **covenant**, or agreement, with Abraham: if Abraham and his descendants would live just and wise lives, then God would look after them for ever and give them a land of their own. This was the Promised Land (which we now call Israel).

The scattering

In the 6th century BCE, many Jews were driven out of their land into Babylon (modern-day Iraq). Some spread to different places. In 70CE, the Romans destroyed **Jerusalem** and the **Temple**, the Jews' holiest place. Many more Jews then fled from their homeland and spread all over Europe. This 'scattering' was known as the **Diaspora**. In the following centuries, the Jews settled in many different countries, where they often suffered prejudice and persecution. In 1948, after the murder of millions of Jews by the German Nazis during World War II, the state of Israel was founded as a Jewish homeland. Today, there are about 15 million Jews. They live all over the world but mostly in the USA, Israel and Europe.

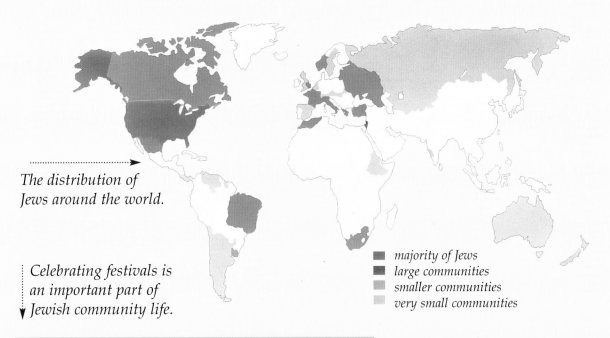

The distribution of Jews around the world.

Celebrating festivals is an important part of Jewish community life.

■ *majority of Jews*
■ *large communities*
■ *smaller communities*
■ *very small communities*

Jewish festivals

There are many Jewish festivals throughout the year. Most remember key times and events from Jewish history. The most important festivals are thousands of years old and are recorded in the **Torah**, the holiest part of the Jewish scriptures. Each festival has its own special customs and ceremonies, which take place at home and in the **synagogue**, the Jewish place of worship.

Keeping Shabbat

habbat is the Jewish day of rest and prayer, as instructed in the Torah, the Jews' holy book. It lasts from dusk on Friday to Saturday night. On *Shabbat*, Jews remember how God created the world in six days, then rested on the seventh. This became *Shabbat*. They also remember how, long ago, their ancestors worked as slaves in Egypt. *Shabbat* is a welcome rest from work. It is a chance to spend time with friends and family, and to think about God.

The plaited challah *bread, eaten on* Shabbat, *reminds Jews of when their ancestors wandered through the desert after their escape from Egypt. On Friday, God sent them two days' worth of* **manna** *(bread) so that they would not have to work on Saturday.*

Shabbat at home

On Friday evening, there is a special *Shabbat* supper at home. Before *Shabbat* begins, the table is laid and the mother of the family lights two or more candles to welcome the *Shabbat* day. Then everyone is given a glass of wine or grape juice, and the father sings a prayer, called *Kiddush*, to thank God for *Shabbat*. In **Hebrew**, *Kiddush* means 'making something holy'.

After lighting the Shabbat *candles, the mother spreads the light with her hands to show joy and peace spreading over the family.*

*A **rabbi** is a teacher who helps people to understand the Torah.*

Shabbat services

On Saturday morning, many Jews attend the main *Shabbat* service in the synagogue. In the middle of the service, the Torah scroll is taken out of the **Ark** (a special cupboard where the scrolls are kept), and the week's reading is chanted. There are prayers and blessings before and after the reading, and a talk by the rabbi.

From the *Kiddush*

'Blessed are You, Lord our God, king of the universe, who makes us holy through doing His commands, and delights in us. Willingly and with love He gives us His holy *Shabbat* to inherit, for it recalls the act of creation. This is the first day of holy gatherings, a reminder of the exodus from Egypt. Because You chose us to be holy among all peoples, willingly and with love You gave Your holy *Shabbat* to inherit. Blessed are You Lord, who makes *Shabbat* holy.'

End of *Shabbat*

At the end of *Shabbat*, a farewell ceremony, called *havdalah*, is held at home and in the synagogue. 'Havdalah' means 'separation'. Blessings are said over a glass of wine, a box of sweet-smelling spices, and a candle. Then everyone takes a deep sniff from the box so that they can carry the fragrance of *Shabbat* into the coming week.

The special havdalah *candle is plaited. It has at least two wicks.*

Rosh Hashanah

The festival of *Rosh Hashanah* (which means 'head of the year'), falls on the first two days of the Jewish month of *Tishri* (September or October). It marks the start of the Jewish New Year. It celebrates the anniversary of the creation of the world, and is also the start of ten important days, called the Ten Days of **Penitence**, which end with *Yom Kippur* (see page 13). This is the most solemn time of the year for Jews, when they think about their lives and behaviour in the past year, and ask God to forgive them for the bad things they have done. They promise to start afresh and to try to do better in the coming year.

Many people send each other cards for Rosh Hashanah.

Celebrating *Rosh Hashanah*

Over *Rosh Hashanah*, Jews eat special meals at home. Among the most popular types of food are slices of apple dipped in honey, and honey cakes. Some Jews serve covered baskets of fruit. Nobody can see what the fruits are, just as nobody can tell what the new year will bring.

At Rosh Hashanah people share apples and honey to wish each other a sweet and happy year.

In the synagogue

During *Rosh Hashanah*, special services are held in the synagogue. There are prayers, songs and Torah readings to help people stop and think about their lives. A musical instrument, called a **shofar**, is blown. The *shofar* is made from a ram's horn which reminds Jews of a story in the Torah about Abraham. He was willing to sacrifice his beloved son, Isaac, to show his love for God. However, at the last minute, God told Abraham to spare Isaac and to kill a ram instead.

Blowing the shofar

The command to blow the *shofar* comes from the Torah. There are many reasons why it is blown. Because it is made from natural materials, it reminds Jews to be honest and natural with God. Its curved shape shows that people's lives are not always straightforward. It also wakes people up, so that they can say sorry for their wrong-doings and feel closer to God. In ancient times, the *shofar* was blown to announce important events, such as the arrival of the king, or to call people to war.

*The notes of the **shofar** are like the sound of a person crying, to show that they are sorry for their wrong-doings and long to return to God.*

Empty pockets

Some Jews perform a special ceremony at *Rosh Hashanah*. They walk to a river, spring or the seashore, and throw breadcrumbs or empty their pockets into the water. This symbolises their sins being washed away, according to the Torah verse: 'And you shall cast all their sins into the depth of the sea.'

························▶

These Jews in California, USA, have written new year's resolutions on pieces of paper, and are placing them in a large bag.

A Rosh Hashanah card

Many Jews exchange greetings cards at *Rosh Hashanah*. You can buy them or try making your own.

To make a Rosh Hashanah *card:*

1. Fold a piece of card in half. Keep the fold on the right because Jewish books open from left to right.

2. Decorate your card with Jewish symbols, such as a *shofar*, **star of David** or a scroll.

3. Then write '*Leshanah Tovah*', or 'Happy New Year', inside.

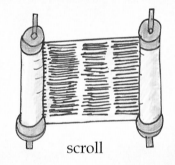

scroll

book

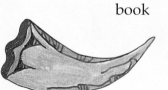

shofar

star of David

Yom Kippur

The tenth Day of Penitence is called *Yom Kippur*, or the Day of Atonement. This is the holiest day of the year when Jews atone, or ask for God's forgiveness, for their wrongs. On the night before *Yom Kippur*, people also say sorry to friends and neighbours with whom they have quarrelled.

Marking *Yom Kippur*

Most Jews spend *Yom Kippur* **fasting** (going without food and drink). Their fast begins at dusk and lasts for about 25 hours until nightfall the next day. This is a way of showing how sorry they are. They believe that, if they are sincerely sorry, God will forgive them.

Jews also go to services in the synagogue at Yom Kippur. At this time, the rabbi and many of the worshippers wear white as a symbol of purity. The Torah scrolls are also covered in white cloth.

At nightfall, a long blast of the *shofar* signals that *Yom Kippur* is over, and marks the end of the fast.

························►

Jews at the Western Wall of the old Temple in Jerusalem praying at Yom Kippur.

A Prayer for *Yom Kippur*

'Hear our voice, Lord our God, show us mercy and compassion, accept our prayers willingly and with love. Turn us back to You, Lord, and we shall return; renew our lives as of old. Hear what we say; understand what we cannot express. May the words of our mouths and the meditations of our hearts be acceptable to You, O Lord, our rock and redeemer.'

Sukkot

our days after *Yom Kippur*, Jews celebrate the festival of *Sukkot*. This usually falls in late September or early October. At *Sukkot*, Jews remember the time, thousands of years ago, when Moses led their ancestors out of slavery in Egypt. (You can read this story on page 22.) After their escape, the Jews wandered through the desert for many years, on their way to the Promised Land. They faced many dangers and hardships but God protected them from harm. *Sukkot* is a happy festival after the fasting and seriousness of *Yom Kippur*.

Pilgrim festivals

Sukkot is one of three festivals, called the **pilgrim festivals**. The other two pilgrim festivals are *Pesach* and *Shavuot*. Long ago, it was the custom at these times for Jews everywhere to travel to Jerusalem to visit the Temple, their most sacred building.

Harvest festival

Sukkot is also a harvest festival. Traditionally in Israel, it marked the end of a long harvest when fruits were picked, grapes were gathered and made into raisins or wine, and olives were picked and pressed to make oil.

These nursery school children are hanging up pictures of fruit to celebrate Sukkot.

Celebrating *Sukkot*

The Hebrew word 'Sukkot' means 'huts' or '**booths**'. For the festival of *Sukkot*, Jews build a hut, called a *sukkah* (plural: *sukkot*) in their garden, on the balcony of their flat, or in the grounds of the synagogue. This reminds them of the flimsy huts and tents in which their ancestors lived during their long journey. A *sukkah* is usually built of wood, with four walls and a roof of leaves or straw. The roof must be thick enough to give shade. But it should also be possible for people to see the sky and think about how much they owe to God.

Jews eat their meals in the sukkah *for the week of the festival. Some invite guests to join them, and even sleep in the* sukkah *as well.*

A model *sukkah*

Try making your own model sukkah:

1. Tie 4 equal length sticks together to make a square. This is your roof frame.

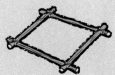

2. Now tie another stick to each corner. These are the poles your *sukkah* will stand on. (Strengthen your *sukkah* by adding more twigs at the base and across the roof.)

3. Cover the roof with leaves, leaving a small gap. Then decorate your *sukkah* with fruit, made from coloured card or even marzipan.

Sukkot in the synagogue

At *Sukkot*, a special service is held in the synagogue. Everyone holds a bundle of branches in their right hand, and a *citron* (a fruit like a lemon) in their left. During the service, people wave the branches to the east, south, west, north, and up and down, while they sing the *Hallel*, or psalms of praise. People also walk round in procession, and chant the *Hoshanot* prayers which ask for God's help in all aspects of life.

*Waving the branches during the **Sukkot** service spreads blessings over everyone.*

Plants for *Sukkot*

Each of the four types of plants used at *Sukkot* has a special meaning. They stand for the parts of the body that can be used to worship God. Together, the plants remind Jews to worship God with their whole body.

*The **lulav**, or date palm, stands for the back, and walking tall and straight.*

*The **aravot**, or willow leaves, stand for the mouth, and speaking truthfully.*

*The **hadassim**, or myrtle leaves, stand for the eyes, and seeing clearly.*

*The **citron** stands for the heart, full of love and kindness.*

Simchat Torah

The festival of *Simchat Torah* falls on the last day of *Sukkot*. In Hebrew, 'Simchat Torah' means 'celebration of the Torah'. Every week, on *Shabbat*, a passage from the Torah is read in the synagogue. The readings start on *Simchat Torah*, at the beginning of the Torah. They end on *Simchat Torah* the following year. Then they begin all over again.

Parading the scrolls at Simchat Torah in Jerusalem.

The Torah

The Torah, or Five Books of Moses, is the most sacred part of the Jewish scriptures. It tells about how the world began, the lives of the first Jews, and contains many laws for Jews to follow.

The words of the Torah are hand-written on scrolls which are kept in the Ark (a special cupboard) in the synagogue.

The Torah scrolls are kept inside cloth covers, decorated with a silver casing.

Parades

Simchat Torah is a joyful festival for Jews. The Torah scrolls are taken out of the Ark (see panel), and paraded seven times around the synagogue. This is called *Hakafot* which means 'circling' or 'going round'. The Torah scrolls are carried at the front, while people sing and dance behind. Children wave special *Simchat Torah* flags, and carry miniature Torah scrolls. They leap to catch sweets thrown by the adults. The sweets are a reminder of the sweetness and goodness of the Torah.

Hanukkah

In November or December, Jews celebrate *Hanukkah*, the festival of lights. *Hanukkah* lasts for eight days and reminds Jews of a great miracle which happened in the Temple of Jerusalem more than 2,000 years ago. The Hebrew word 'Hanukkah' means 'dedication' because this was when the Jews dedicated their Temple to God again.

The miracle of *Hanukkah*

Long ago, Israel was invaded by the Syrian Greeks. Their king, Antiochus, wanted the Jews to worship the Greek gods. He took over their Temple, and allowed the lamp to go out. Some brave Jews, called the Maccabees, refused to give up their religion and drove the Greeks out. However, when they tried to relight the Temple lamp, there was only enough oil to last for one day. Then a miracle happened. God kept the lamp burning for eight days, until more oil could be fetched. This showed the Jews that God is always with them, even in difficult times.

The special Hanukkah candlestick is placed in the window so that everyone can see it.

Festival of light

Hanukkah, Jews light a special candlestick, called a **hanukiah**. It reminds them of this miracle. There is space for eight candles, with a ninth candle, called the *shamash*, to light them with. The eight candles stand for the eight nights of *Hanukkah*. One candle is lit on the first night, two on the second night, three on the third, and so on. Special prayers and blessings are said before each candle is lit.

Fried foods

It is the custom to eat fried foods at *Hanukkah*, such as crispy potato *latkes*, or sticky *blintzes* (doughnuts). *Latkes* are small pancakes made from grated potato and onion. They are eaten with apple sauce and soured cream. The oil in which the food is fried is a reminder of the oil in the Temple lamp.

Sticky jam doughnuts are a favourite Hanukkah *treat.*

Dreidel
(spinning tops)
with six sides

A traditio...
dreidel has
four sides,
like this one.

Playing games

During *Hanukkah*, people play traditional games, such as *dreidel*. A *dreidel* is a spinning top with four sides. Each side is marked with a Hebrew letter. The letters are the initials of the words 'A great miracle happened there'. The game is usually played for a pot of raisins or chocolate coins.

To play dreidel:
Each player takes turns to spin the top and see which letter it lands on. Each letter is also an instruction. It tells the player to take all the coins or raisins in the pot, take half, take none or put one in.

Purim

The Jewish festival of *Purim* falls in February or March. It remembers the great danger faced by the Jews who lived in Persia (modern Iraq) more than 2,400 years ago, and celebrates the triumph of good over evil. The word 'Purim' comes from a Hebrew word meaning 'drawing lots', or choosing something at random.

...............▶

Purim is a time of great joy and celebration.

Haman's pockets

One of the special foods eaten at *Purim* is called *Hamantaschen*, or 'Haman's pockets'. These are triangular pastries, stuffed with honey, fruit and poppy seeds. They are also called Haman's ears because of their shape.

Queen Esther

The story of *Purim* comes from the Book of Esther in the Jewish Bible. King Ahasuerus of Persia was married to a girl called Esther, but he did not know that she was Jewish. The king's chief minister, Haman, hated the Jews, and gave an order to have them all killed on a date he picked out at random. Esther's uncle, Mordecai, asked Esther for help. At great risk, Esther invited the king and Haman to have dinner with her. She told the king that she was Jewish and that Haman wanted to kill her and her people. Furious, the king had Haman put to death and the Jews were saved.

In the synagogue

The synagogue is usually a quiet, serious place. At *Purim*, however, things are very different. During a special *Purim* service, the story of Queen Esther is read out loud from the **Megillah** scroll. Whenever wicked Haman's name is read, everyone tries to drown it out by booing, hissing, stamping their feet and shaking rattles, called *greggors*. This is a way of getting rid of evil.

These Israeli children are wearing colourful fancy dress costumes to celebrate Purim.

A *greggor*

To make your own Purim greggor:

1. Half fill an empty soft drink can with buttons, beads or beans.

2. Cut a piece of cardboard to cover the end of the can which has the pouring hole. Glue it in place.

3. Cut two circles from felt and glue them to the ends. Then cover the rest of the can with felt. Don't forget to shake your *greggor* every time you hear Haman's name!

Parties and plays

Purim is a day filled with celebrations. All over the Jewish world, adults and children dress up in fancy dress, often as characters from the story. There are prizes for the best costumes.

Children take part in *Purim* plays and parades, and go to *Purim* parties. There are games, singing and dancing, and plenty of delicious things to eat and drink.

But *Purim* is also a time for charity. Many Jews give food and money to the poor so that they can enjoy the festival, too.

Pesach

In late March or April, Jews everywhere celebrate the festival of *Pesach*, or Passover. This is one of the three pilgrim festivals (see page 14), and one of the most important times in the Jewish year. At *Pesach*, Jews remember how God helped their ancestors to escape from Egypt thousands of years ago, and thank God for their freedom.

The Story of *Pesach*

Long ago, the Jews lived in ancient Egypt, where they worked as slaves for the Egyptian pharaoh, or king. God told Moses to lead the Jews from their slavery.

Many times, Moses went to the pharaoh and asked him to let the Jews go. Each time, the pharaoh refused. Then God sent ten terrible plagues to punish the Egyptians.

Finally, to stop the Egyptians' suffering, the pharaoh ordered the Jews to leave, and allowed them to begin their journey to the Promised Land of Israel.

boils

blood

hail

frogs

locusts

lice

darkness

wild beasts

death of first-born sons

disease

The ten plagues of Egypt eventually persuaded the Egyptian pharaoh to allow the Jews to leave Egypt and travel to their own land.

The parting of the Sea of Reeds

Moses led the Jews into the desert where God guided them by day and night. But, some days later, the pharaoh changed his mind and sent his army after them. The Jews found themselves trapped between a lake, called the Sea of Reeds, and the Egyptian soldiers.

Even then, God came to their rescue. He sent a wind which parted the sea so that the Jews could cross safely. Then the water closed again, drowning the Egyptians who tried to follow.

Jewish children singing in the synagogue.

A Song for Pesach

The Dayenu *is a song which Jews sing at* Pesach. *The Hebrew word 'Dayenu' means 'it would be enough for us'. The song lists all the good things which God did for the Jews after their escape from Egypt, and thanks God for them. You can read some of the verses below:*

Had He brought us out of Egypt
And not fed us in the desert,
Brought us out of Egypt,
Well then – Dayenu!

Had He brought us to Mount Sinai,
And not given us the Torah,
Brought us to Mount Sinai,
Well then – Dayenu!

Had He given us the Torah,
And not led us into Israel,
Given us the Torah,
Well then – Dayenu!

Had He led us into Israel
And not given us the prophets,
Led us into Israel,
Well then – Dayenu!

Celebrating Pesach

The days before *Pesach* are very busy as preparations for the week-long festival begin. The whole house is spring-cleaned before families gather together to share the celebrations.

For supper on the first night of Pesach, Jews eat special symbolic foods from a seder plate to remind them of the life of the Jews in Egypt.

Bitter herbs, such as horseradish, are reminders of the bitterness of slavery.

A roasted egg and lamb bone are reminders of offerings made to God.

A dish of salty water is a symbol of the slaves' sweat and tears.

A green vegetable, such as parsley or lettuce, is a sign of spring and new life.

Spring-cleaning

The spring-cleaning is to remove any last crumbs of *hametz*. This means anything that is made with yeast or leavened (risen) dough, such as bread, cakes and biscuits. The Jews had to leave Egypt in such a hurry that they baked their bread without letting the dough rise, so the bread was thin and flat. Some people wash their everyday crockery and cutlery, in case they have any *hametz* on them. Then they put them away and use a special set for *Pesach*.

Charoset *is a mixture of nuts, apples and wine. It stands for the cement which the Jews used in buildings for their Egyptian masters.*

Pesach supper

On the first night of *Pesach*, families sit down to enjoy a special meal. It is called the *seder*. In Hebrew, 'seder' means 'order', because everything happens in a set order. The *seder* begins with the youngest person at the table asking four questions about the past. The answers are read from the **Haggadah**, a book which tells the story of *Pesach*. As the story is read, people taste the different foods laid on the special *seder* plate (see left). During the course of the meal, only the egg and the lamb bone are not eaten.

◄·············

The youngest person asks the four questions.

Charoset

To make a dish of charoset, *you will need:*

2 eating apples
a handful of mixed nuts
a handful of raisins
a pinch of cinnamon
2 tablespoons of grape juice

1. Peel and core the apples. Grate them or chop them into small pieces.
2. Break up the nuts. You can do this by putting them in a plastic bag and crushing them with a rolling pin.
3. Mix all the ingredients together.

Hunt the *afikomen*

Thin, flat bread called *matzah* is eaten at *Pesach*. It is a reminder of the bread the Jews took with them when they fled (see left). At the beginning of the *seder*, a *matzah* is broken in two. One piece is left on the table. The other, larger piece is called the *afikomen*. It is hidden somewhere in the room. After the meal, the children hunt for the *afikomen*. The *seder* meal cannot end until the *afikomen* has been found, so the finder gets a prize.

·························►

Breaking the matzah *in two.*

Shavuot

The third pilgrim festival is *Shavuot*, which falls in May or June. 'Shavuot' is the Hebrew word for 'weeks' because the festival falls seven weeks after *Pesach*. At this time, the Jews celebrate how God gave the Torah and the Ten Commandments to Moses on **Mount Sinai**. This happened long ago, while the Jews were wandering in the desert after their escape from Egypt. The Torah, or Five Books of Moses, became the Jews' most sacred text. Jews look upon the Torah, as God's greatest gift to them.

On the evening before Shavuot, *some Jews stay up all night studying the Torah.*

The Ten Commandments

The Ten Commandments are ten rules which Jews use as a guide for how God wants them to live.

1. I am the Lord your God, who brought you out of Egypt, from slavery.
2. Worship no other gods but me.
3. Do not use God's name falsely.
4. Keep the *Shabbat* day holy.
5. Respect your father and mother.
6. You shall not kill.
7. You shall not commit adultery.
8. You shall not steal.
9. You shall not tell lies about others.
10. You shall not be jealous of other people's possessions.

From the Torah

'In the beginning God created the heaven and earth. And the earth was without form, and void; and darkness was upon the face of the deep. And the Spirit of God moved upon the face of the waters. And God said, Let there be light, and there was light. And God saw the light, that it was good, and God divided the light from the darkness. And God called the light Day, and the darkness he called Night. And the evening and the morning were the first day.'

(Genesis 1, verses 1–5)

A Torah scroll

Try making your own hand-written Torah scroll:

1. Write out the first verses of the Torah (see above) on a long sheet of paper, or on several sheets, glued together.

2. Decorate the ends of two long cardboard tubes (from the insides of rolls of aluminium foil or food wrap).

3. Glue the ends of the paper to the tubes. Leave the glue to dry, then roll the paper on to the tubes.

4. Tie your scrolls with a brightly coloured ribbon. Then unroll them when you are ready to read.

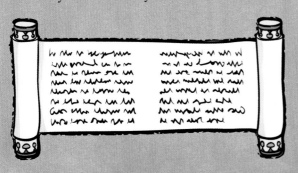

▲ *Decorating a synagogue with flowers.*

Celebrating *Shavuot*

At *Shavuot* services in the synagogue, passages are read from the Torah telling how the Ten Commandments were given. People also hear the story of Ruth, a non-Jew, who married a Jewish husband. When her husband died, she continued to follow his religion, and the teachings of the Torah. Synagogues are decorated with flowers and fruit, because *Shavuot* is a harvest festival. It is also said that, when the Torah was given to Moses, Mount Sinai burst into flower.

Festival Calendar

Date	Jewish month	Festival
1	Tishri	Rosh Hashanah
10	Tishri	Yom Kippur
15	Tishri	Sukkot
		Simchat Torah
25	Kislev	Hanukkah
14	Adar	Purim
15	Nisan	Pesach (Passover)
6	Sivan	Shavuot

Jewish months

The months of the Jewish year are:

Tishri	(September/October)
Heshvan	(October/November)
Kislev	(November/December)
Tevet	(December/January)
Sh'vat	(January/February)
Adar	(February/March)
Nisan	(March/April)
Iyyar	(April/May)
Sivan	(May/June)
Tamuz	(June/July)
Av	(July/August)
Elul	(August/September)

Glossary

Abraham	The father of the Jewish people who made a covenant with God.
Ark	A special cupboard in the synagogue in which the Torah scrolls are kept.
Booth	A temporary shelter.
Covenant	An agreement made between God and the Jews.
Diaspora	The 'scattering' of the Jews around the world.
Fasting	Going without food or water.
Haggadah	A text which gives the order of service for the festival of *Pesach*.
Hanukiah	A nine-branched candlestick used at *Hanukkah*.
Hebrew	The language in which the Jewish holy books are written. The language of modern Israel.
Hebrews	A nomadic people who lived in the Middle East about 4,000 years ago. They became the Jews.
Jerusalem	A city in Israel which is sacred to the Jews.
Manna	Food which God sent from heaven to feed the Jews as they wandered in the desert.
Megillah	A scroll telling the story of Esther.
Mount Sinai	The mountain on which God gave the Torah to Moses.
Penitence	Putting right things that you have done wrong.
Pilgrim festivals	The three Jewish festivals of *Pesach*, *Shavuot* and *Sukkot*.
Rabbi	A Jewish teacher and spiritual leader.
Shabbat	The Jewish day of rest and prayer.
Shofar	A ram's horn blown at Jewish festivals.
Star of David	A six-pointed star which has become a symbol of the Jews. It is named after David, the great Jewish king.
Synagogue	A building in which Jews meet and worship.
Temple	The ancient Jewish temple in Jerusalem. It was the holiest building for the Jews.
Torah	The holiest teachings of the Jews. The Torah is also known as the Five Books of Moses.

Further Resources

Books

A World of Festivals: Passover
David Rose and Gill Rose, Evans Brothers, 1997

Celebrations! Hanukkah
Mandy Ross, Heinemann, 2001

Storyteller: Jewish Stories
Anita Ganeri, Evans Brothers, 2001

Celebration!
Barnabas and Annabel Kindersley, Dorling Kindersley, 1997

Festivals in World Religions
The Shap Working Party on World Religions in Education, 1998

World Religions: Judaism
Angela Wood, Franklin Watts 1999

Beliefs and Cultures: Jewish
Monica Stoppleman, Franklin Watts, 1996

Websites

www.festivals.com
Festivals, holy days and holidays.

www.new-year.co.uk/jewish
Facts, background and activities for Rosh Hashanah.

www.jewish.co.uk/festivals
The Jewish calendar and its festivals

www.everythingjewish.com
Jewish festivals and all aspects of Judaism.

www.join.org.au/a-to-z.htm
An A-to-Z of Jewish Australia.

www.wej.com.au
More info about Jewish Australia.

Index